Twenty First Century Blues

CRAB ORCHARD SERIES IN POETRY

Editor's Selection

Twenty First Century Blues

Richard Cecil

Crab Orchard Review

Southern Illinois University Press

CARBONDALE

Printed in the United States of America

07   06   05   04   4   3   2   1

The Crab Orchard Series in Poetry is a joint publishing venture of Southern Illinois University Press and *Crab Orchard Review*. This series has been made possible by the generous support of the Office of the President of Southern Illinois University and the Office of the Vice Chancellor for Academic Affairs and Provost at Southern Illinois University Carbondale.

Crab Orchard Series in Poetry Editor: Jon Tribble

Library of Congress Cataloging-in-Publication Data

Cecil, Richard, 1944–
Twenty first century blues / Richard Cecil.
p. cm. — (Crab Orchard series in poetry)
I. Title. II. Crab Orchard series in poetry
PS3553. E32T94 2004
811'.54—dc22
ISBN 0-8093-2596-9 (cloth : alk. paper)
ISBN 0-8093-2597-7 (pbk. : alk. paper)   2004002474

For Maura,

and for Olive and Oleander,

the sweetest cats

who ever lived

Contents

Acknowledgments

Poems in this book first appeared in the following publications:

Another Chicago Magazine—"Fool's Gold"

American Poetry Review—"A Lesson in Generosity," "Albi Cathedral," "Lament for the Makers"

Atlanta Review—"Internal Exile"

Crazyhorse—"Anti Ode to Autumn," "Twenty First Century Blues"

Diner—"Holy Sonnet"

Ellipsis—"November's Advice"

Flying Island—"A Christmas Poem"

ForPoetry.com—"Summer Diet"

Green Mountains Review—"A Rare Bird"

The Journal—"Letter of Recommendation"

Louisville Review—"Portrait of Five Women and a Cat"

MacGuffin—"Meditation on a Half-Line of Shakespeare's"

Montserrat Review—"Flying Home"

Notre Dame Review—"As You Like It"

Southern Review—"Written in Exile"

Southern Indiana Review—"Package Tour"

Tampa Review—"Contrary Elegy"

Virginia Quarterly Review—"Limbo"

One

Lament
for
the
Makers

Lament for the Makers

Thank god the twentieth century is over.
It started great, with Yeats and Robert Frost
abandoning the artificial diction
of nineteenth-century poetry and writing
lines that thoughtful people might have spoken
after they'd kept silent for a long time.
Then World War I wrung great poems from
doomed soldiers at the front, like Wilfred Owen,
and transformed T. S. Eliot's "The Waste-Land"
from an obscurely personal lament
for psycho-sexual failure and neurosis
into a moving dirge for pre-war Europe's
disintegration into twenties chaos.
But Europe in the thirties could inspire
no poetry as eloquent as cries
of anguish by the victims of the Nazis,
so modernists like Stevens plugged their ears
and turned for inspiration to Ideas,
which they worked into satisfying Texts
suitable as subjects for a Thesis.
They left the second war to novelists,
young soldiers like James Jones and Norman Mailer,
whose minor masterpieces sold to the Movies,
which turned their tragic views of History
into star vehicles for Donna Reed.
Meanwhile soldier poets wrote odes and sapphics
based on dead forms borrowed from the Greeks
while laying plans to translate *The Aeneid*.
Jarrell's "The Death of the Ball Turret Gunner"—
five lines of iambic pentameter—
is World War II's only major poem.
But in the forties greatness wasn't dead.
Robert Lowell, if he hadn't failed
the Navy's eye test when he volunteered,

would've been the Wilfred Owen of his war
instead of the celebrity protester
who burned his 4-F draft card after Dresden's
incineration by the Allies' firebombs.
Instead of getting drowned or kamikazeed
assaulting some bleak atoll near Japan,
he thrived in jail and afterwards discovered
that his authentic muse was Mania,
his Yaddo an asylum called McClean's.
He founded, without meaning to, the school
of Confessionals, who, in the sixties, raced
like rich Twits in the Monty Python skit
toward the finish line, their suicides,
which fixed their place in literary history
and guaranteed space in anthologies.
Their flashy deaths obscured much finer work
by Robert Hayden, buried in the South
beneath a four-course load at a black college,
whose Elegies for friends and foster parents
trapped in his childhood ghetto in Detroit
turned Lowell's sour rich kid memoirs inside out,
and by Lowell's great friend Bishop, who holed up
for decades with her girlfriend in Brazil
writing formal narratives and lyrics,
ignoring world and literary politics
while Lowell cranked out his "Notebook" free verse sonnets
chronicling his Viet Nam war protests,
his infidelities and second divorce.
Then one by one, these three great poets died
twenty years before the century ended,
leaving only Larkin, almost silent,
grinding out his mordant, funny lyrics
at the rate of two or three a year
on the other side of the Atlantic.
Then he died and left the pages blank
for us to fill in—for if you're reading this,
statistics say that you must be a poet,

4

one of the many thousands who apply
for NEAs biannually and are denied.
Or have you been awarded one or two?
Well, then, maybe you're the major poet
whose works will light the twenty-first century up
as soon as jealous rivals like me die
and critics gain the necessary distance.
Or maybe I'm the secretly great voice
almost drowned out by all that background noise,
twenty thousand singers tuning up,
almost all of them way out of key.
But sister, brother, our bones will turn to dust
long before the new anthologies
replace crap written by X and Y and Z
with the major works of you and me,
so I'm leaving blank the end of this lament
for you to fill with your own elegies:

Catechism

Suppose there were a Heaven—not the Holy
Howling Choir that Dante conjured up
and sentenced sycophants to endless worship
for wasting lifetimes pleading with the Bully
to let them kiss His ass eternally,
but the Resurrection of Emily Dickinson,
where everything Death stole and every person,
flowers, pets, lovers, friends and family,
gets restored unharmed to us—what then?
Should thinking that the Thief makes restitution
reconcile His victims to the crime?
Would Morris purring endlessly in Heaven,
Stan grinning, my mother fussing, be compensation
for the agony of losing them in time?

Albi Cathedral

Though eager to check out The Last Judgment
painted on the wall behind the altar,
I paused to peer up at the stained glass windows
shooting blue and ruby beams like lasers
through the gloom. At first they seemed abstract,
just random puzzle pieces glued with lead,
but stepping closer, I made figures out.
A praying man bent towards a chopping block
in panel one; in panel two his soul
flew up to heaven through his severed neck.
In panel three a woman gazed serenely
skyward while two soldiers cut her breasts off.
In panel four she held them on a platter
like a hostess serving up hors d'oeuvres.
These must be scenes from lives of famous martyrs,
I thought, although I didn't have a clue
who any of them were until I reached
the final window in the aisle and saw
St. Lawrence being roasted on his griddle.
He's the one, nuns said, who, dying, quipped,
"I'm done on this side; it's time to turn me over!"
That really cracked me up in the third grade—
the only martyr with a sense of humor
I'd heard of till I walked this aisle and saw
beheaded, de-breasted, crucified, and broiled
martyrs smiling down from every window
while their tormentors frowned—weary floggers,
a headsman cursing the bluntness of his ax.
But when I came at last to The Last Judgment
in shadow at the end of the long aisle
and played my flashlight down from God's left hand
towards souls condemned to bright red flames of Hell,
I saw the right relationship restored
between the tortured and their torturers.

Sinners' eyes bulged and their tongues thrust out
with agony as they were plunged in oil
boiling in a cauldron hanging over
a pile of blazing logs poked up by tridents
and stoked by bellows pumped by eager claws
of grinning Devils who enjoyed their work.
No poker-faced or frowning demons plied
their cats-o'-nine-tails over sinners' backs,
and not one of their victims hid the anguish
of being driven down into the pit.
This painter's got a flair for the grimace,
I thought. Each twisted face I beamed on
looked like the portrait of an enemy
thrust into Hell with gusto by an artist
inspired as Dante by lust for revenge.
But Dante worked in exile, bitterly.
Some Bishop had commissioned this Inferno
behind the altar, which the congregation
faced to receive instruction every Sunday
in what awaited them the day they died
naturally, if they obeyed the Word,
or harrowed by fire and sword if they rebelled
like many thousand local heretics
whose stamping out this church commemorated.
And there they are, the Albigensians,
some purple-robed priest thundered from the pulpit,
pointing towards the wall of howling sinners
who died in agony for their wrong faith
eight hundred years ago. And now the martyrs
smile down on them from their sparkling windows
because they suffered torture for the right one.
I turned and left, having learned my lesson:
I've lost my soul, if I ever had one.

Limbo

One afternoon this summer in Assisi
I stood where experts stood a few weeks later
craning their necks to estimate quake damage
to the Church of St. Francis's frescoed vault
when it collapsed in an aftershock and crushed them.

As pains shot through my stiff neck, I complained,
Why paint a masterpiece it hurts to look at?
To ease a tingling nerve, I leaned way back
like a Calypso dancer slipping under
the Limbo stick his grinning partners lower.

All at once, I wasn't in Assisi
near the end of the Second Millennium
checking out eight-hundred-year-old art
by masters of the Early Renaissance
soon to become a pile of bloody plaster.

I fell through a crack in my consciousness
and landed, drunk, at a party in the sixties.
"How looow can you gooo," sang Harry Belafonte
on the stereo while my friends clapped their hands
as I tried to bob under the broom handle.

I flexed my knees and spread my feet apart
until I teetered on the edge of balance,
but the broomstick hovered way too low
for me to slide my heaving chest beneath it,
so I fell backwards on the green shag carpet

and lay there panting while the ceiling spun.
"You're doomed to go to limbo when you die,"
called out a girl I loved more than champagne.
Her rich voice mingled with the throbbing bongos.
She was a singer. When did I last see her?

That was the year that Johnson bombed Hanoi
and my draft board rescinded my deferment.
All I remember's watching her recede
through a bus window as I pulled away,
thinking *death won't be as bad as this.*

It didn't cross my mind that I'd survive
the war and her rejection, fall in love
with someone taller and more beautiful
who'd blot out recollection of her face
for more than a quarter century,

until this afternoon in Italy
when a pinched nerve in my spine replayed my past
like a needle dropped onto a dusty record
called *The Limbo Rock.* I straightened up
and walked back out into the rain-slicked streets

which paved a secret flaw beneath Assisi
soon to open up beneath the church
and bring its heaven's painted saints and angels
down on experts sent to check the damage
because they knew all of its ancient flaws.

Like lovers staring at a brand new portrait
of someone they lost many years before,
they'd notice new, heartbreaking imperfections
not there when they took their last longing look.
The cracks must have moved them to near-despair:

they'd have to work whole lifetimes to restore them.
Then the floor trembled, bringing down the ceiling
on them and all their futile aspirations.
And what do I remember of that lost treasure?
The face of someone who's forgotten mine.

Let's Pretend

Keats didn't die in his bed in Rome.
Instead he staggered down the Spanish Steps,
sat by the Trevi Fountain and inhaled
enough Italian air to cure his lungs.
Recuperating, he wrote a sonnet sequence
describing his miraculous recovery
called *The Ship of Death Sets Sail Without Me*,
which sold enough to pay its printing costs.
Flushed with new hope, he composed *Hail, Sun!*—
two dozen mediocre odes that praised
Italian wine and food and dusky skin.
Hail, Sun! drew raves from the same Scot reviewer
who tore to pieces his first book of poems.
It sold ten thousand copies back in London
to desperate, pasty people trapped in England.
"I'm at my height—it's time to write my Epic,"
he wrote in his journal. First he proposed
to stretch *Hyperion* to epic length,
but his publisher wrote back that classic myth
was guaranteed to kill sales of a book,
even with nude Venus on its cover.
Then it dawned on Keats—the Arthur legend!
War and infidelity and religion!
Milton had chosen Arthur as the hero
of his English epic two centuries before,
then changed his mind and made his hero Satan
when he went blind and England turned against him.
"Now Milton's dead and popular," Keats thought.
"I'll dedicate my *Fall of Gwyenevere*
in three volumes, vellum bound, to him."
He chuckled to himself as he envisioned
Wordsworth turning pale when he got word
of the *Fall of Gwyenevere*'s huge sales—
Wordsworth, who called himself the modern Milton,

who'd sneered that Keats's early work was "pretty"!
Keats rubbed his hands and dipped his sharpened quill
in purple ink the color of Bordeaux.
"Her velvet bodice trimmed with ermine—no,
I'd better start *The fog-hung chalky cliffs*
to make sure every English reader knows
it's England where this epic's taking place."
But suddenly a Zeus-flung thunderbolt
splits his roof and zaps Keats Posthumous,
the Frankenstein invented by my brain
to prove that failure's greater than success.

Anti Ode to Autumn

"Three hot meals a day, a whirlpool tub,
and stunning ocean views from every seat
of our thousand-square-foot cafeteria,"
sounds pretty good to me, but what assistance
does your "Assisted Living Plan" provide?
I don't yet need help to get out of bed
and dress and feed my cats and walk to campus
and climb three flights to my Intro to Lit Class,
but lately I've experienced this numbness
in my brain when I read famous poems.
My students' eyes glaze over as I drone
lines like *I heard a Fly Buzz when I died,*
That time of year thou mayest in me behold,
And now I live, and now my life is done,
all highlighted years ago in yellow
in third- and fourth-hand Used anthologies
because they always show up on my Final—
Part I (60 Points): Identification.
No one gets their authors or their titles
wrong any more except the chronic sleepers
whose faint snores in the silences that follow
my asking if the class has any questions
torment me with desire to lay my head
down on my desk and take an hour's nap.

So, as you see, the assistance I need living
at this stage of my life is not a nurse
to wheel me to and from my comfy room,
but a PhD/Veterinary Doctor
to take care of my classes and my cats
while I cash in a chunk of future pension,
fly to Paris, and rent a one-star *chambre*
with no heat hissing through its radiators
to stop my shivering and make me drowsy

while I read poets mummified by Norton
to find out which works live, like Frost's "Out Out,"
and which are fossils, like Eliot's Quartets.
Which of Shakespeare's sycophantic sonnets
praising his patron-boyfriend would I take
if I were editor of the *New Yorker*
and he sent me all hundred fifty four?
Which of the seventeen hundred and seventy five
obsessive-repetitious meditations
in Emily Dickinson's *Collected Poems*
blows my mind the way "I died for Beauty"
did when I first sneered down at it in High School,
expecting genteel lines by an old lady,
and read that corpse-eye-view of stony death?
Is "John Donne as fake as a TV preacher
and Gerard Manley Hopkins just a whiner
in their flashy, overwrought religious sonnets,"
as my best student wrote on this year's Final,
Part II (40 points): Compare & Contrast
"Batter My Heart" with "I Feel the Fell of Dark"?

But thanks so much for sending your brochure.
As I glance at its cover illustration—
the grizzled skulls of two Residents
staring through your restaurant's plate glass
at churning surf turned orange by a sunset,
I think of Matthew Arnold's "Dover Beach,"
"a poem where this old guy who's shacked up
with his girlfriend on the coast gets depressed
because the tide of faith is going out."
The tide of my faith, too, is on the ebb—
I'd trade a week of snorkeling in Key Largo
for the need to ever read or explain again
Stevens' "Idea of Order at Key West,"
"where two men, one a Cuban named Ramon,
follow this woman singer down the beach
trying hard to make sense of her song
till it gets dark, and they give up and go home."

Here, at my home, it's getting darker too.
Gathering gangs of Florida-bound birds
squawk in the trees all up and down my block
although the mercury's still in the 90's,
and my calendar's black-circled day approaches
when I'll stuff *Paradise Lost* into my sack
and trudge up to my freshman Great Books class.
They'll shuffle and cough as I open to page 20,
where Satan welcomes his burning host to Hell,
and clear my throat, and croak "HAIL HORRORS, HAIL!"
as an Air France jet with many empty seats
screams overhead on its way east to Europe,
and startled birds take off for Vero Beach,
where the stunning ocean views from every seat
of your thousand-square-foot cafeteria
take in a beach that symbolizes nothing
and, even when it's lashed by hurricanes,
refuses to reveal its secret meaning.

Discuss "Divine Justice in *The Inferno*"

I'm sorry class—my cat peed on my briefcase,
which I set down too near her litter box
in my study where she sleeps on my old socks.
Well written as they are, your Dante essays
stink, literally, as does my praise
scrawled in your soggy margins: "Good illustration!"
"Here you show superb imagination!"
and my all-purpose writing cheer: "well phrased!"
So, would you please accept this group citation
for excellence in analyzing Dante,
as the army issues a unit commendation
for bravery? You all deserve an "A"
for writing down a rational explanation
of a revenge-crazed poet's view of judgment day.

Fool's Gold

Alphonse Daudet's Man with a Golden Brain
breaks off a nugget to repay his parents
for saving him from being stolen young,
then starts to mine his head for precious lumps
to finance his expensive dissipations
until one bleary dawn he catches sight
of his blank stare reflected from his mirror,
which frightens him so much that he turns miser
and takes a manual job to hoard his brain.
But his best friend, let in on his secret,
robs him in his sleep of half his remnant,
and then one day he meets a bird-like blonde
and starts to dig out bits to buy her presents.
No, she doesn't leave him empty-headed
after spending his last golden thought—
that's the story Baudelaire would tell.
She marries him, delights in his rich gifts,
but dies in just two years of who knows what?
exactly like a bird and leaves him gold
enough to buy *"Une belle interrement,"*
her casket coach drawn by four plumed black stallions.
After her splendid funeral he stumbles
through nameless streets until at dusk he's lured
to a lighted showcase window where he spots
a pair of down-lined, sky-blue satin shoes.
"She'll love these," he mumbles, shouldering through
the boutique's door as he claws at his skull,
then thrusts his bloody nails at the screaming clerk.

"So what's the moral of this writer's fable?"
I wonder as I cross out "shoes," write "boots,"
then change it back to "shoes" because *bottines*
are more precisely "half boots" or "high top shoes,"
but I don't want to drag in connotations

of "old-fashioned" or of "L. L. Bean."
The shoes are not down-lined, they're trimmed with swan's
feathers, but I couldn't squeeze that image
into one line—I'd have to slop it over
and dissipate the force of the attraction
of something blue and soft lit by a spotlight
on the empty-headed Man who'd spent his brain
on greedy parents, false friends, and his wife.
The Man, of course, was Daudet himself,
living on the bits of brain he sold,
and also me and you, since only writers
read in our time, which is why our brains—
—my brain—is barely worth its weight in lead.
Nobody but me mines my mental vein,
which yields me more, not less, as I dig deeper.
Or am I simply heaping piles of mica,
brainlessly confusing it with gold?
Either way, Daudet's metaphor
does not apply to me. My mother's dead;
she died poor. No friends steal my ideas
because I have no friends, and my wife mines
her own brain's ore and sells it for much more.
So Daudet's martyred Man is one more fable
reinforcing writers' selfishness,
as if we flinty bastards needed lessons
in how to hoard and hold on to our treasure.
But how I envy Daudet's spendthrift hero,
pursued and hounded for his precious talent.

The Funeral Director: Against Cremation

Travel experts say, since views don't change,
whether of blank brick walls or of the Alps,
that paying extra for them is a waste.
But when you take your permanent vacation
from eating, sleeping, working, making love,

a discount for no vista's not a bargain.
You *must* splurge on a windy hilltop plot
and top it with a granite obelisk
carved only with your name & dates
since epigraphs go in and out of fashion.

While you're at it, buy the tru-seal coffin
with the hundred year leak-proof guarantee,
which only costs two thousand more than caskets
that let grave water in. Five cents a day
will save your corpse a century from rot.

But after that, only your works can save you—
not necessarily good works. Take Lenin,
mummified and glass encased for tourists
to gape at as they shuffle past.
He's still on show although his cult's died out.

His corpse is all that's left of Leninism;
his writings pulped to make recycled paper
for Christmas cards, the Czar he shot's a saint,
but he's not rolling over in his grave.
He's grinning in his see-through mausoleum,

just as you'll be if your works are remembered
even though they're misinterpreted.
But burned and scattered ashes draw no fans.
Inter yourself where people want to stand
gazing in the distance. Raise a stone

for them to spray paint tributes to you on:
The King Lives! We still love you Jim!
Next century, your works will be in fashion.
You'll be the next Emily Dickinson.
Don't cheat the mobs who'll throng your gorgeous tomb.

The Worst Day of the Year

for depressing poets

The Santas, Frosties, wise men and grazing reindeer
have been unplugged and repacked in the basements
of houses stripped of strings of Christmas lights.
Halloween, Thanksgiving, Christmas, New Year's—
the holidays that mark the year's decline
into the pit of winter are surpassed,
and what they pointed towards is finally here.
Unmarked on calendars, it falls this year
on the day my fever hits 102,
and, looking out my filthy panes, I see
Wallace Stevens's Nothing That Is There
lit by Dickinson's Oppressive Slant of Light.
Every branch is bare; the sky's blank,
as if not clouded over, but erased.
Wind-blown beer cans skitter down the street;
bundled walkers lurch by, dragged by dogs;
cars thump past, blaring ugly music.

When greeting cards for this day get invented,
the views framed by my bedroom's filthy windows
will be engraved on boxed sets by Hallmark:
First Street Strewn with Salt; Back Yard Trash.
Inside, cheerless lines from Hopkins's sonnets—
"Despair, Despair, Despair, Despair!"—or Larkin's
"Unresting Death, one whole day nearer now"
or something creepy out of Baudelaire
will say what this day means to me and you
more eloquently than you or I could say
because, bad as things are, we're gripped by hope
that after this, every day is up.
Already, sodden birds are practicing
their mating calls for Valentines, and crocuses

are stirring just below the muddy surface
like land mines waiting for the sun to set them off.
The weeds of expectation are springing up,
poisoning my crop of misery,
since, if this is as bad as things can get,
that means everything is looking up
unless you're dead and your desperation's final,
in which case, "No worse, there is none!" is really true,
and, lucky you, your whining is immortal.

Portrait of Five Women and a Cat

Five women stare down from my study walls.
The thin, unsmiling lips and rigid jaws
of Charlotte, Anne, and Emily Brontë
charge me with being lazy. They seem to say
with their gleaming gray and hazel eyes,
"replace that purring cat stretched on your thighs
with your writing pad and pen, you lazy shirker!
If we three hadn't been relentless workers
we'd be less famous than that drunken lout,
our brother, who painted us." Meanwhile "The Mute"
nailed to the door of my closet full of suits,
unworn since I quit trying to look nice,
stares out of her placid, marble face
coldly at Raphael, whom Father paid
to paint her velvet gown trimmed with brocade.
It's several centuries since death wrung groans
from her swan-like throat, and Raphael's just bones,
but art this coldly perfect never dies,
so now it's me her painted eyes despise.
I love her rich contempt, but when I gaze
too long at her, my blood begins to freeze.
That's when I turn to "Housewife from Pompeii,"
a cardboard copy of a gold and gray
mosaic buried by volcanic ash,
which covered up the house of Mrs. X
at the same time that it preserved her face.
She's homely but dolled up—earrings and necklace
distract from asymmetrically drawn cheeks.
I can't tell from this distance which was weak—
her chin, or the art that mimicked it in stone.
Yet her portrait moves me the most. Her moan
of pain and fear in 79 A.D.
is terrifyingly audible to me.
I want to save her—not from oblivion,

which this poor picture has already done—
but from her awful death. Bourgeois Lady,
isn't it true that you ran away
with the craftsman that your rich old husband hired
to show you in your costliest attire?
Tell me your faithlessness saved you from fire
and broke your husband's heart so that he sighed,
gazing at your thick eyebrows, and died
the week before Vesuvius' eruption
strangled people, but "saved from Time's corruption"
their houses, knickknacks, pins, and powder puffs
like some Dutch painter, so in love with stuff
he labors weeks to paint a high lace ruff
by layering a thousand minute strokes,
not noticing the lovely neck it chokes.
That kind of artist brags that his great work
rescues his trivial subjects from the dark,
like nameless women Shakespeare "immortalized."
But not all artists' egos are king-sized.
Nobody knows which Pompeiin pressed
gray stones together to outline X's chest;
the Brontës' portrait was painted by a drunk
who creased it up and thrust it in a trunk,
and Raphael's great passion is submerged in
the icy surface of that frigid Virgin.
These women on my walls move me more than
the art that saved them from oblivion.
If art could really save, I'd save this cat
on my lap, asleep, that the Brontës frown at;
I'd chip "The Mute" from that iceberg of art
and set her back on earth with a beating heart;
I'd give the Brontës back their brilliant brains,
this time with sets of lungs as tough as bronze.

The Writing Requirement

Sign up now! You're guaranteed a place
in Undergraduate Creative Writing
if you register before lack of enrollment
signals the computer to delete it
and switch its teacher to Intensive Writing,
which everyone at State's required to take.
In Intensive Writing you'll be forced
to write or purchase essays on dull subjects,
such as poems that your prof tells you are great,
while in Creative Writing you'll compose
poems that your prof's required to praise
even though they aren't very good.
Chances are, your prof writes poems, too—
when he/she isn't writing praise on poems—
poems not much better than your own
judging by the number of rejections
they're garnering from little magazines
edited by out-of-state grad students
taught by professor poets whose own work's
rejected by grad students here at State.
This means that poetry's the only art
where the master is in thrall to the apprentice,
which may explain why so few freshman plan
to take up poetry as their profession,
and why poetry professors seem depressed,
and rarely show up for their office hours.
They're busy writing novels that they hope
will be made into major motion pictures,
which people who hate poems love to watch.
With the fortune that these novels make, they plan
to quit teaching and take up writing poems
they will not try to place in magazines.
Instead, they plan to tie them up with ribbon
and bury them in drawers, like amateurs,

like freshmen who don't take Creative Writing,
or who cut the class on Publication.
But first, the novel. So hurry, undergraduates.
Sign up before the bidding war begins
for *The Passionate Life of Emily Dickinson.*

To the Poet Who Skipped
My Reading & Died

Now that you've felt the force of Richard's curse,
how do you like the taste of graveyard dirt?
I didn't mean to make your bad heart burst
but those I hate seem always to get hurt.

Once dead, I don't suppose I'd be obsessed
with who or what killed me, but you kept score,
knew who counted and who didn't, so my guess
is that you ache to know what you died for.

Well, I'll be glad to share this with you, B—
when adding up the chances I'd have power
to do you good or harm, you shorted me.
Oh, you saved yourself a tedious half an hour

of listening to me droning on and on,
but listen to me drone now that you're gone.

A Letter to William Butler Yeats

Imagine Yeats if Maud Gonne whispered *yes*
the first time he asked her to marry him,
and then moved with him out of crazy Ireland
to Indiana where, on St. Patrick's day,
they sipped Irish Coffee by their fire
and sang along with John McCormack records.
Deprived of his wellsprings of lust and rage,
what would spur Yeats to passionate utterance?
Nostalgia for the peat bogs of his youth,
for grimy cities and rain-sodden fields?
Scorn for U.S. elections where a scoundrel
vied with a fool to become his President?
Or would his English Department's politics—
for how else could a poet in the States
make a living if he didn't teach?—
stir him into bitter eloquence?
Without a Celtic Twilight to obscure
or Easter Rising to throw a lurid glare
across life's paths, which all lead to the tomb,
Yeats, I'd like to think, would think like me
that colleagues out to derail his career
were worthy of his high artistic passion.
Denied advancement to Associate
with its attendant thousand-dollar raise
because his Service ranked just "Adequate"
although his Publications were "Outstanding,"
wouldn't Yeats put down his Rosicrucian
pamphlets and pick up his poison pen?
Instead of "Sailing to Byzantium,"
about escaping artist-hating Ireland
by soaring on wings of imagination
out of the place and time that he was mired in,
wouldn't Yeats have written "Screwed Again"?
Or would he prudently have volunteered

to serve on the Curriculum Committee,
which studies the Teaching of Creative Writing?
Oh, William Butler Yeats, please advise me,
if you can spare time from your busy schedule
of lying night and day in Sligo Churchyard—
How can I make *my* petty rage immortal?

Two

There's No Place Like Home

Package Tour

Included in "Authentic Indiana"
is your choice of a Rent-A-Wreck used car
or round-trip transfers to the Greyhound station,
plus seven nights at the Motel Downtowner,
next door to Doc Johnson's Marital Aids
and three blocks from the Big Red Liquor Store.
From day one to day eight you're on your own
unless you choose the optional excursion
to Stonehenge Winery just outside town,
where, ever since frost killed off all the vines,
tank trucks have hauled in California grapes
to vats where they're transformed to Hoosier wine,
which you can buy a bottle of on Sunday
thanks to a loophole in the local blue laws.
On your way home from Stonehenge, you may choose
to visit Hoosier History Mini-Golf,
where every hole's a reconstruction of
a fire or flood or local massacre
(all history here's a record of disaster),
or, if you're in a hurry, you may short-cut
through the trailer park and Kroger's lot
back to your cozy room at the Downtowner,
pop the cork on your Gewurtztraminer,
and pour yourself an aperitif before
you cross the street to dine at Waffle House.
"Glow, Little Glow Worm" will be playing low
through speakers of the booth you slide into.
You'll start to hum along unconsciously
as you scan the egg-stained, laminated menu,
until you hear yourself, and stop, and wonder
how you came to know words of this oldie
no DJ ever played in your lifetime.
Did Mother sing it while she squirted Joy
on plastic dishes soaking in the sink?

Was it the theme song of some '50s quiz show
subliminally imbedded in your brain?
Impossible to guess the source of stuff
you never tried to learn, but simply know,
or think you know until you read one day
that the continent of America was discovered
by British sailors five years before Columbus,
who thought that Cuba was the coast of China,
and kept on saying so until he died.
But travel teaches lessons even falser.
Remember that great week you spent in Maui?
The patio where you sipped wine and watched
the sunset every day's been swept away
by a tidal wave of new development,
and the young shark you swam with like a brother
has doubled in size and tripled in appetite.
You can't revisit a place where you were happy,
as you can't re-love someone you loved and left,
except in memory revived by drink.
But now and then you have to get away
or else you'll sink in quicksands of nostalgia.
But where? The "Islands of the Sirens" Cruise
is booked in blocks by the AARP;
the London/Paris/Rome/Vienna fling
spends more time in the air than on the ground;
the post-repression mini-tour of China
requires you to forget atrocities.
But if you choose "Authentic Indiana"
you'll cure your case of traveler's delusion
that any place is better than your home,
unless, of course, your home is Indiana,
in which case you live only in your dreams.

There's No Place Like Home

Ninety-seven of one hundred retirees
stay in hellholes where work forced them to waste
the best part of their lives. Two-thirds of the rest
sell their big houses and move locally,
not to the sun-drenched desert or the sea,
but to a smaller and much cheaper place
with little upkeep and with zero grass
to mow so they can rest until they die.

Just one moves out of state, and of that one
percent one in a thousand leaves the country—
takes off from St. Louis, lands in Orly
and never, never sends a postcard home.
So no one knows if old exiles are happy—
just that they never come back to Missouri.

Almost an Apartment in Antibes

Today I'm going to exercise my option
to not reserve this sea-view studio
that's featured on the Riviera web page
by not converting eleven thousand dollars
in money market savings into francs
to wire-transfer to Credit Lyonnaise.
Though I've clicked "HOLD," I do not plan to "BUY"
tomorrow's cheapest Air France flight to Nice;
I won't be flying handcuffed to a suitcase
stuffed with cash withdrawn from IRAs
less ten percent tax penalty for not
allowing them to grow until I'm sixty.
No agent's going to meet me at the airport
and drive me twelve kilometers to town
exclaiming in franglais about how wise
I am to buy now with my soaring dollars
this undervalued Euro property.
"*Oui!*" I won't reply when she asks me
if it's my plan to live here every summer
and visit every Christmas till I quit
my U.S. job and move to France to die.
"And would you like me to find you a tenant
to occupy your space when you are absent?"
"*Non, Madame,* I want to leave it vacant,
waiting for me like a sailor's wife
who gazes out to sea all winter long,
until her husband's ship appears at last
tacking past the cape into the harbor,
even if he's like Odysseus,
who didn't make it back for twenty years,"
is more or less what I won't say to her
as she conducts me up her office stairs
to sign the papers drawn by her *notaire.*
Commissions, Fees, Percentages and Tax

add up to nothing on this non-transaction.
Today's the day I didn't take the plunge
into the bottomless Mediterranean Sea
of currency speculation and foreign debt.
Tomorrow, I'll move to my permanent residence,
this house I've merely camped in nineteen years
and, stranded forever on Indiana's shore,
admire its breathtaking vistas of regret.

Evolution in Indiana

I thought that species took ten thousand years
to gradually evolve new strategies
to deal with shifts in climate or environment,
but after two snow-free years in a row
the local robins all at once decided
to winter here instead of flying south.
I watched them pace my lawn in late November,
debating like small Hamlets with their instincts:
"It's way past time to migrate; why haven't I?"
Since, every fall, a few old, feeble ones
decide they'd rather risk starvation here
than drop dead of fatigue in Alabama,
at first I thought it was their kind I glimpsed
rummaging discarded Christmas trees
for grubs and squabbling with the greedy squirrels
stealing birdseed from my neighbor's feeder.
But then, one drizzly January walk,
I spotted dozens, looking sleek and healthy,
plucking worms who'd washed up on my sidewalk.
Why *here,* where I was forced to grub for money
all winter long, when they could fly away,
I wondered as they hopped out of my path.
Does flying hurt so much they'd rather shiver
and see the sun once every other week
than perch in palms swayed by an ocean breeze?
If I had wings, I'd use them . . . and on and on
I muttered as I trudged around the block
in pointless circles, just for exercise,
hands thrust into my pockets, arms tight to sides,
like some huge flightless bird, while overhead
the most successful members of my species
winged effortlessly southward in high Boeings
invisible from our side of the clouds—
we well-fed and hard-working flock of Dodos.

Heaven

At the end of sunny days, our evening swim
is followed by mixed drinks beside the pool
served either in frosted glasses, slim and cool,
fizzy with tonic and 94-proof gin,
or else in tulip cups with salted rims
outside and golden tequila within. No fools
start tossing around beach balls, against the rules,
or cranking up rock music. *The Harp of O'Carolin,*
a CD wafting through the open window
that overlooks the patio dining set,
is calling us to uncork the Bordeaux,
fill up the ruby glass Venetian goblets,
and glide into our places for the show:
Moonrise Sonata scored for silver crickets.

As You Like It

Suppressing thoughts of the French Riviera
in February, grading stacks of essays
on "Mockery of Travelers in *As You Like It*,"
I notice that the speech all papers quote—
"Look you lisp and wear strange suits, disable
all the benefits of your own country,
be out of love with your nativity"—
is spoken by a joking Rosalind
in prose instead of in blank verse, which means

that Shakespeare didn't mean the words he wrote
to draw roars of approval from the cheap seats,
who loved to hear that travel to bright worlds
beyond their reach would spoil their native virtue.
"Let those silly nobles in the stalls
waste time and money traveling south to sip
sour wine and float in Gondolas—
we'd rather huddle by our fires at home
washing cold joints down with warm beer."
It's always awful stuff that locals praise—
the lutefisk, the barbeque, the haggis—

just as it's the worst of foreign countries
that cosmopolitans prefer to home—
rocky, narrow, topless *plages* in France
to wide, clean sandy beaches in New Jersey;
ski-trail blighted slopes in the Swiss Alps
to unspoiled Rocky Mountain wilderness.
With cautious drivers, toll-free Interstates,
gas less than half the price of gas in Europe
and a thousand miles of semi-tropic coasts,
America's where it makes sense to travel,

which must be why I almost never do.
I'd rather go nowhere than drive a Chevy
to someplace warm where natives all speak English.
I'd rather hole up in my freezing room
with one wall covered by a map of France
and others hung with prints from St. Moritz
dreaming of my next authentic trip
to the mouthwash-colored Mediterranean Sea,
where the quality of life's precisely measured
by stars affixed to the hotel's marquee.

Oh, how Rosalind would have sneered at me,
a person born in a land so gigantic
that hating winter's not unpatriotic
since getting warm requires no foreign trip.
Palms and condos rise beside the Gulf
a long day's drive or short domestic flight
from where I sit and brood in Indiana,
my gloomy little country in a country,
shunned by travelers and by the winter sun—
like Shakespeare's England, which is as we like it.

Let's Go!

"Nothing good comes from the Morvan,
neither good people nor a good wine,"
say neighbors of this no-star region,
according to *Guide Michelin*.
Its stony ground supports no vines
or any crop but oaks and pines.
In Avallon, Morvan's museum,
as darkly lit as a mausoleum,
exhibits bric-a-brac so worthless
most visitors can not suppress
sneers like those on waiters' faces
as they serve the fools who waste
their time in Avallon's cafés,
where service, many tourists say,
is worse than on Champs-Elysées.
But that's the solitary likeness
between dull Avallon and Paris,
groan the Parisians on their way
south who stop here for the day
when driving to the Riviera.
Like Yankees crossing the Dakotas
in loaded vans or cramped Toyotas,
they book bad rooms here in advance
since they're afraid to take the chance
of sleeping in their Citroens,
or, worse, in woods where black bears den,
protected from inroads of men
by land that's part of Burgundy
but grows no vines, just nuts and berries.
In Morvan there are no gourmets,
jazz festivals, or passion plays—
a black hole in the tourist's map
without a single tourist trap.
Can a place so much like home exist

less than two hundred miles from Paris?
I wonder as I jot down "Morvan"
on the projected route I plan
to follow if I get the chance
to escape next year on Air France
from my woodsy Midwest province,
though—write this down—I like it fine:
both its good people and its bad wine.

A Rare Bird

The trouble with American resorts?
Americans! They're big and slow and speak
their language loudly with a native accent
that sounds so much like mine it makes me cringe.
Their evening cries of "Hey, Hon! Take a look
at this gorgeous sunset!" wafting toward me
from their rented seaside balconies
depress me, for I've just chirped the same phrase
to my mate, who's responded with her call,
"Ah, yes!" as she's stepped through the sliding door
to perch beside me at the condo's railing.

It's hard to tell the finest of the species
from ordinary members of a flock,
since doing anything that's truly different
such as fly north when all the rest fly south
proves fatal ninety-nine times in a hundred,
like driving on the left in the U.S.
The safe way to feel special when you travel
is to shun your own kind and to mingle
with foreigners in neutral territories,
such as Swiss paths where Japanese and Brits
wave walking sticks and greet you with *"Gross Gott!"*

Take that cardinal who just now landed
in my dogwood to pluck berries with the starlings.
Although he's not a rare bird in my yard,
he looks like a king dining with his peasants.
He's thinking, if birds think, "It's great to eat
with foreigners whose chatter makes no sense."
But what exactly are those starlings cackling?
Satirical remarks about red feathers,
pointed heads, and black lone-ranger masks?
What difference, as long as he can't translate?
Meaningless conversation soothes like Muzak.

Last summer I had lunch in Umbria
with a friend who scowled at a table lifting glasses.
"Asshole Americans!—that's what they're toasting."
"No, John," I said, although I'm monolingual,
"That sounds to me like 'Thank God we're Italian!'"
"Well, thank God we're not," he said and clinked
his water glass against my glass of wine.
"Thank God!" I echoed him, drinking deeply
of the cheap delicious Soave I'd despise
if Italy were home instead of heaven,
and America's where I'd fly to be foreign.

Where Am I?

Beyond the waves that lap the sandy beaches
my balcony looks down on, there must be
no distant shoreline, only open sea
that stretches toward the west until it reaches
the sky to make an infinite horizon,
which the sun sinks into with a hiss
of surf as afternoon and evening kiss
good night and sky turns on its constellations.

The only sounds allowed besides the surf
are cries of gulls and very distant swimmers
and snapping flags so twisted by the wind
it's impossible to say who rules this turf,
the Kingdom of the Endless Perfect Summers,
which I move to every winter in my mind.

The Tower of Babel

Antibes

Chased off the pavement by a motor scooter,
I picked up the tourist map I'd dropped
and studied my route with a sinking heart:
yes, my seaside condo *was* uphill.
I turned my back on the Mediterranean
and rolled my suitcase up a boulevard
choked with eight lanes of horn-honking traffic
until at last I sighted RESIDEAL,
a blue sign on a pole beside a high rise,
the "four-star residence beside the sea"
I'd salivated over like a porn site
all winter long on the Internet.
But when I stepped into its barren lobby,
I saw that what had looked like polished marble
and mahogany on my computer screen
were sanded concrete and wood-grain Formica.
Therefore I wasn't too surprised to find
that my Grand Studio was not as posh
as it appeared on screen. Bare as a cell,
it overlooked the SNCF station
so that I could watch trains arrive and leave
and compare them to my Thomas Cook timetable.
Beyond the tracks, a mile downhill, the sea
dimly shimmered through the orange air.
Those four stars must stand for the dialects
of Eastern Europe that the desk clerks speak,
I muttered as I ransacked kitchen shelves
for a spatula and corkscrew and found none.
No salt shaker and no coffee filters,
no foil or sandwich wrap or frying pans.
The renters who preceded me left nothing,
as if they were retreating in a war

and I were the advancing enemy.
Finally, I gave up frisking drawers
and made a list of stuff I'd have to buy
at the Mono Prix downtown and haul uphill—
a fan to stir un-air-conditioned air
and blow away the fumes of cigarettes
of my chain-smoking poker-playing neighbors;
plastic forks and knives; an omelet pan;
some eggs and cheese and a bottle of champagne.
That night, exhausted from my double climb,
I sat outside in my ripped canvas chair
sipping Mumm's from a plastic flute
while listening to the murmur of Croatian,
Ukrainian and Polish, Czech and Finnish—
languages I recognized by instinct
since I, too, was a sun-starved inlander
driven towards the sea by my blood's tide.
I rose and leaned as far out as I dared
over the shaky rail to catch a glimpse
of the lights of yachts of multi-millionaires
twinkling through the filthy, humid air,
then raised my crummy glass full of great wine
to toast our tower's polylingual revels
by oil-slicked sea beneath the smoggy stars.

Internal Exile

Although most people I know were condemned
years ago by Judge Necessity
to life in condos near a freeway exit
convenient to their twice-a-day commutes
through traffic jams to jobs that they dislike,
they didn't bury their heads in their hands
and cry "Oh, no!" when sentence was pronounced:
Forty years accounting in Duluth!
or *Tenure at Southwest Missouri State!*
Instead, they mumbled, *not bad. It could be worse,*
when the bailiff, Fate, led them away
to Personnel to fill out payroll forms
and have their smiling ID photos snapped.
And that's what they still mumble every morning
just before their snooze alarms go off
when Fluffy nuzzles them out of their dreams
of making out with movie stars on beaches.
They rise at five a.m. and feed their cats
and drive to work and work and drive back home
and feed their cats and eat and fall asleep
while watching Evening News's fresh disasters—
blown-up bodies littering a desert
fought over for the last three thousand years,
and smashed-to-pieces million-dollar houses
built on islands swept by hurricanes.
It's soothing to watch news about the places
where people literally will die to live
when you live someplace with no attractions—
mountains, coastline, history—like here,
where none aspire to live, though many do.
"A great place to work, with no distractions"
is how my interviewer first described it
nineteen years ago, when he hired me.
And, though he moved the day that he retired

to his dream house in the uplands with a vista,
he wasn't lying—working's better here
and easier than trying to have fun.
Is that the way it is where you're stuck, too?

Written in Exile

Eve and Adam leased a Maui Condo
one mile south of Kapalaua Bay
just off lower Honoapiilani Highway.
Through their wall-of-glass sliding window,
they stepped out to their lanai at six or so
to toast the fireball sunset every day
with frosty flutes of Napa Chardonnay,
while their CD player crooned hits of Don Ho,
underscored by crashing surf and cries
of surfers riding in their final waves.
On their last night, they stared at Molokai's
black hills, which shadowed distant leper's graves.
"Jesus Christ, Eve, this is Paradise!"
Next day they flew to glum Midwestern lives.

Three

A Lesson in Generosity

Falling Off the Wagon

Swimming with Pacific sharks
off a Maui reef last March
seemed more relaxing than my drink
with colleagues at a bar last night
to celebrate our victory
over my former friend and ally.
Fifteen years of abstinence
must've spoiled my taste for liquor,
for, though I bottoms-upped a scotch
and chased it with a pint of stout
without falling on my face,
the stuff, which used to make me babble,
caused me, instead, to go dead quiet,
the way two puffs of pure hashish
did the only time I smoked it.

That was the year that "Sergeant Pepper"
hit the charts and I got drafted
after the U.S. bombed Hanoi.
On leave awaiting travel orders,
I visited a friend who moved
to New York City after he
got certified unfit for service
by a friendly, leftist doctor
for his "tendency toward migraine."
He threw a party in my honor,
inviting all his cool new friends
in editing and publishing,
who passed the pipe around to me.
The penalty for smoking hash
back then was five to fifteen years,
so possibly my fantasy
that the tall guy with the Afro
who handed me the tiny pipe

was an informer or a Narc
wasn't paranoid, just prudent.
But chances are the loud and rapid
seditious talk about The War
was only normal New York speech
raised in volume to be heard
above Ravi Shankar's sitar
whining on the stereo,
not raised to get picked up on tape
to be re-played at my court martial.
But I sat cross-legged and tight-lipped,
pretending to be lost in thought,
meditating with the music.
Is this what's called a 'bad trip'?
I wondered as I glanced around
at all my friend's friends grinning faces.

Faces which, by now, resemble
those lined and weathered smiling faces
I sat across the table from
last night, avoiding eye contact
by staring at my frosted mug,
examining my bitten nails,
and looking up at the mounted moose head
whose kindly brown eyes met my stare.
"What are you doing here?" he said,
accusing me with his mild gaze
of belonging to the human race,
which doesn't charge and lock antlers
when it fights over territory,
but sneaks up with high-powered rifles,
long-range bombs, and guided missiles,
and celebrates its victories
not trumpeting alone in triumph
but howling with the pack, "a toast!"
No use telling that dead moose
that if the other side had won

my former friend, without remorse,
would be sitting in my place
clinking glasses with his gang
and shouting jubilant remarks
about me and my loser "friends,"
while I sat home before my fire
isolated and depressed,
which is as close to virtuous
as I've ever come in life.
I almost wish the bastard won!
Next time I drink I'll drink alone.

A Christmas Poem

"Brother, can you spare some change?" I shook
my head, then tried to hustle out of range
before the old panhandler took advantage
of my denial to berate my cheapness.
"Hey, Mister Scrooge! You saving up for Christmas?"
Ouch! What details in my grubby outfit
told him that though he was the better dressed
in almost new work boots and jeans and jacket
doled out to him from the Goodwill basket,
I'd once forked up a fair amount of money
for my frayed jeans and worn-out running shoes?
Instinctively I patted my pants pocket
to make sure that it still bulged with my wallet,
stuffed with credit cards and souvenirs—
a ten-year-old "Admit One" into Graceland,
and several expired IDs to jobs
I worked a few weeks or a month or year,
but not a dollar or a five or ten
or twenty if I'd wanted to impress him
and even if he'd meant "change" literally,
I didn't have a nickel, dime or quarter
rattling in the pocket with my keys
and mini-flashlight to make out the keyhole
when I walk home unsteady after dark.
He must've had more cash on him than I did,
and if we traded clothes I'd be the gainer—
shouldn't I have been accosting him?
Oh, but I had powerful rich friends:
Mr. MasterCard and Mrs. Visa,
and my favorite, MAC, who slips me fifty
every time I ask, without a protest
or even a sarcastic reference
to all the other times I've hit him up.
So credit was the only difference

between me and my brother on the street,
and if I'd been a little bit like Jesus,
I would've hit the corner ATM
for cash to give him, and if I had been Jesus,
I'd have handed him my card and code,
but since I'm me, and flat broke besides,
I trudged home through the slush and wrote this poem.

Holy Sonnet

Since you've complained in writing every day,
described the errors in My universe
in trimeter, tetrameter, and blank verse
and gotten no response, you've come to pay
not much attention to the stuff I say
in My unsigned rejection slips to thee:
"I am impressed by the futility
of your desire. Try Me again someday."

Given the volume of My correspondence
I can't reply, every time you curse,
personally by hurling thunderbolts,
or bless you now and then with an acceptance.
Keep trying, though. Your efforts are no worse
then those of millions of your kind, all dolts.

On Being Asked to Contribute to
The Idiot's Guide to Poetry

Write a poem in Hiawatha rhythm.

Looking into restroom mirrors,
I don't notice FOOL or NITWIT
spelled in big block letters backwards
like a bowling team's insignia
on my chest, and not too many
people I meet out in public
sneer or chuckle openly.
But adults know that it's unsafe
to make fun of friends or strangers
so they play at Halloween
in reverse, all year long, by
slipping blandly normal faces
over grinning Bozo clown-masks.
My guess is that what they make out
written over me's the same thing
I'd see written over them if
I looked up from the minefield
that I tip-toe through in public
dodging tossed banana peels,
lunging back from stoplight runners
towards the safety of the curb.
DUMMY! KLUTZ! are not expressions
I shout at retreating tail lights
of successful puddle splashers
who throw muddy gutter water
all the way across the sidewalk
so that there's nowhere to leap.
You can guess the words I holler
once I'm sure the STUPID ASSHOLE
driver isn't big and scary.
You're as wise as me, or wiser.

You're no YAHOO; you're no DUFUS;
You know that a poem's worthless
and that how to write one's useless
knowledge if you call it knowledge
to know how to measure words out
on a page in drumbeat rhythm—
futile work for little money
(zero money's what I was paid
for this exercise you're reading)
Why not save your eighteen-fifty
for a LAMEBRAIN'S GUIDE TO GOLFING
or Elizabeth Bishop's POEMS.
Please re-shelve this Idiot's How-To-
Do what does not need to be done.
Buy yourself a café latte,
open Bishop to "The Man-Moth,"
leave me singing to myself, please
here on page 221,
Dumb-da Dumb-da Dummy-Dumb.

Sailing to Pesaro

Sois sage, o ma Douleur
—Baudelaire

Tides of adrenaline surge through my brain
as Nitwit's nasty e-mail lights my screen:
"My long experience," "call into question,"
"executive decision"—dead phrases float
on turgid currents of his primer syntax
like fish killed by a discharge of raw sewage.
I'll push "reply" and blast that stupid bastard.
NO! Be calm, my soul. Take my hand.
I'll pull you from that boiling froth of rage
and climb with you this hill of memories
we mounded up last month in Italy.
Look—there's the Ristorante by the sea.
Inside, a live accordion plays polkas
old couples dance to; out on the patio,
young teens who look like stars in *West Side Story*
shyly flirt and clown at the next table
while we watch sunset and sip Lambrusco.
After the last drop of our whole carafe,
we tip our waiter thousands of lire extra
and stroll unsteadily the beach called Wanda
back to the Hotel Flying and sweet sleep.
But first, let's sit out on our balcony
in canvas chairs and watch the Adriatic
wavelessly reflect the waning moon,
which waxed two weeks before in Sicily.
It gilded tenements that filled the window
of our one-star Albergo in Palermo,
turning slums into a fairyland;
then it shone full on Agrigento's temples,
still standing after two millennia
of catastrophic earthquakes and attacks

by Christian fundamentalist fanatics
filled with certainty and blind to beauty,
just like Nitwit. NO! Calm down, Soul.
Let's watch the mirrored moon shine on the water.
Each night after this it will grow slimmer.
The evening our return flight touches down
it will have shrunk into a silver sliver
shimmering in the bug-spattered windshield
of the stretch limo hauling us back home
to routine rivalry, and petty malice
that gleams dully through Nitwit's clichés.
Yet, the instant his e-mail lit my screen,
it moved me more than Yeats' greatest poem,
in which he sails away from lusty neighbors,
driven by the passions in their veins,
and lands his soul, stripped of his aging body,
on the shores of an artificial country,
where it can sing to bloodless men and ladies.
Not me. Not us, I mean, unsoulful Soul.
We like our skin burned olive by the sun.
We love both the black-haired, black-eyed young
and the silver-haired old couples dancing
half-drunk at nightfall to an accordion
to which we sang off-key accompaniment
in broken phrases of Italian—
music unfit for a soul to sing
to lords and ladies, or, God knows, a king.
But come on, Soul, let's hum "These Foolish Things,"
close our eyes, reconjure the waning moon.
But how, you wonder, will we reply to N.?
Keep singing, Soul; sip your sparkling wine
while I eclipse his message with DELETE.

2001: HAL, Meet Dell

They can't think, but they can do mischief.
—Stanley Kubrick

My Dell's learned how to turn herself back on!
I clicked on "Shut Down" and her screen went blank,
but when I came back to work at my desk
I heard Dell hum and saw her On light glow.

I clicked on "Shut Down" and her screen went blank,
so I pushed Dell's on/off button once again.
I heard Dell hum and saw the orange glow
of her monitor-in-standby warning light,

so I pushed Dell's on/off button once again.
Her pixels crackled and her Power light went out.
But her monitor-in-standby warning light,
next morning, was still glowing. I punched Off.

Her pixels crackled and her Power light went out.
But when I came back to work at my desk
next morning, it was glowing. Why punch Off?
My Dell's learned how to turn herself back on.

Summer Faculty Enrichment
Grant Application

If Odysseus had started home from Troy
that hot September day ten years ago
when I first circled desks and called the roll,
he'd have arrived on Ithaca by now,
been reunited with his son and wife,
killed all her suitors and disloyal servants,
and be beginning to feel a little bored
with family life, so why should I feel guilty
that I'm less eager now to teach Great Books
than when I first held up the tourist map
ripped from my battered Baedeker Red Guide
and traced the Hero's path from Turkey's coast
to the island chain on the western side of Greece?

Yet I'm no closer to my journey's end
than when I was appointed Permanent
Part-time Unpromotable Assistant Professor
assigned to teach dead Greek and Roman poets
whose works I can read only in translation.
The chair who hired me thought I was an expert
in the poetry of my contemporaries
and therefore never asked me to teach them,
fearing I'd demand a hefty raise
if asked to lecture on the stuff I knew.
But her successor doesn't need to fear
my competence in what once was my field—

I've read Fitzgerald's Homer night and day
for years, but nothing by still-breathing poets
except the books friends send with dedications.
I know more, now, about the competitions
for brazen shields, tripods and slave girls
in Homer's and in Virgil's funeral games

than about book contests run by Pitt and Yale,
and I can quote more of Dido's lament
after she's abandoned by Aeneas
before she stabs herself on her own bier
than I can quote from poems Plath wrote after
Ted Hughes left her, before she gassed herself.

But I'm not boasting of this ignorance,
which links me to the poet-hating world.
It's just that now it's too late to catch up
with the twenty thousand writers who've emerged
since I first started frantically preparing
my introductory talk, "The World of Homer,"
based on a trip that I once took to Greece,
where I researched the island of Mykonos
looking for a room that didn't rock
all night to "I Can't Get No Satisfaction,"
then sailed to Crete to study Minoan ruins,
but studied, instead, menus penned in German.

But now my memory of that trip has faded.
When I trace Odysseus's path through the Aegean,
I no longer feel the throb of diesel engines
propelling my rusty World War Landing Ship
through darkness I feared dawn wouldn't interrupt
if I shut my eyes and the helmsman nodded off.
I feel, instead, the steady shush of oars
plied by Phaeacian sailors while their guest
sleeps dreamlessly beside the pile of treasure
they gave him for reciting his account
of his ten-year journey, called *The Odyssey*,
full of lies, but metrically exact.

They paid a fortune for a contemporary poem!
No wonder Phaeacia's a legendary island!
For ten years, while teaching summer school
I've researched guide books in Borders with no success,

looking for the Club Med Island in the Aegean
whose topless beach Odysseus washed up on,
whose top hotel was built on the foundations
that once held up the palace of a king
who supported poets four thousand years before
the National Endowment for the Arts dried up.
This summer, could you please grant me ten thousand dollars
to search, in person, for the ruins of my dead art?

Meditation on a Half-Line of Shakespeare's

Until I put myself up for promotion
against the customs of my sub-department
where I'm permanently assigned a junior rank,
I never understood why Hamlet answered,
when asked what's wrong by spying Rosencrantz,
"Sir, I lack advancement." It's suicide
for princes to admit they would be kings,
so why would Hamlet say that his distemper
stemmed from resentment at being outmaneuvered
by Claudius, who stole the throne of Denmark?
I used to guess that Hamlet wished to die
but not to break the law against self-slaughter,
and, therefore, goaded Claudius to murder.
But then, why not just whisper in Roz's ear,
"because I know my uncle killed my father"?
Treason's treason, I used to tell myself—
I'd choose to die for truth, not pointless fiction.
But now that I have been denied advancement
on technical & on procedural grounds
by Rosencrantz and Guildenstern's descendants,
it seems to me I've solved the Hamlet riddle:
tell every fool who asks your dearest secret
that you desire to rise beyond their level;
they'll never guess there's murder at your heart.

Letter of Recommendation

X was a joy to work with.
Quiet, but never sullen,
X talked when talking was called for
and didn't when it was not.
X rarely was absent or late
and turned in written work
always on time, spelled right,
and grammatically correct.
X showed imagination
when imagination was called for
and didn't when it was not.
X got along with others,
and others got along with X
in a non-competitive environment.
In every category
on your ratings sheet except
"Manual Dexterity,"
of which I have no knowledge,
X ranks in the top ten percent
of the Xs I have worked with
and far exceeds myself
in Potential for Advancement.
In two or three years at most,
X will surpass me in earnings
and soon will be writing letters
for the Ys who'll strive to advance
by doing the work assigned them
cheerfully, and on time,
and who will write letters in turn
for the twenty-first-century Zs
who'll manage in my absence,
when my small power to boost
or retard careers is dispersed
with the dust of my rotted corpse.

Please carve this epitaph
in italics on my stone
as my recommendation to them,
though they never asked for one:
Be spendthrift in your praise
of others when you write;
hoard irony for yourself.

A Lesson in Generosity

"How do you like my work?"
no writer asks a writer,
as mothers never ask mothers
"How do you like my child?"
An arrogant jerk would say
"I don't," but everyone else
would stare at their shoes and lie
to conceal their indifference
to stuff they didn't make.
But what about "generous" writers
who chair the grants committees
that fund apprentice work
by the young and powerless?
Who praise contemporaries
in Arts Page interviews,
lay wreaths on teacher's graves,
and promote their students like agents?
You know the one I mean.
Groans never pass her lips
when Pulitzers are announced,
and he's the only panelist
who doesn't deplore the present
degeneration of craft.
No, I'm not talking about
back-scratching book reviewers
who write blurbs for each other
or professional introducers
whose job requires them to praise,
I'm talking about that writer
who pressed a competitor's novel
in my hands and said "read this!"
Was his the subtlest scam,
to give praise to the needy
(it wasn't much of a book)

and thereby increase, not diminish
his store of personal credit?
"Giving gives to the giver"
in his case wasn't gibberish
since the well of praise is bottomless,
unlike the well of money.
It's fed by a limitless source,
so its level never drops
no matter how many buckets
get hauled up and poured out.
So why not give away
something that costs nothing
which everyone wants so badly
since everyone else is so stingy
you'll earn a reputation
for generosity for free?
Try practicing in a mirror
saying, "I like your book"
over and over until
no hint of a sneer curls your lips,
no irony edges your tone,
your eyes meet your eyes squarely.
Now turn towards me and say it.
Thank you. I like yours too.

Four

Twenty
First
Century
Blues

Contrary Elegy

Two things you can't write about are the death of pets
and junior high school love.

Week after week, the black cat up the street
did not trot to the sidewalk for some pats
on his broad back when I passed by his yard
on walks I took just for my health, I thought.

But after one month of not seeing him
curled on his porch, or stretched out on his lawn,
I realized that *he* was why I walked
the same route after supper every night,

pulse quickening as I approached his hedge,
just as it did on junior high school dates
when I caught sight of my first girlfriend's house,
until one night she told me "I don't love you"

and shut her gate behind her with a click.
For months I walked past her fence every evening,
lit up a cigarette outside her gate,
and drew in the deep ache of nicotine.

I prayed that she'd spot me in the streetlight
exhaling poison smoke and cry down: *Don't!*
but she never did. No slender silhouette
appeared in her bright window all those weeks

I walked past, gazing up, until at last
my painful hoping turned into despair,
which turned into indifference so slowly
that I still wake up sobbing when she leaves me

in dreams three decades later. That's the pain
I felt when I passed Blackie's empty yard—
a dull, unfocused aching in my chest—
until one night his people, hauling groceries

out of their van, detoured across their lawn
to say that they had seen me from their window
stopping by their hedge to look for Blackie—
they thought they ought to tell me he was dead.

So now, when I walk past his big blue house
I know that he won't spot me and trot out
crying for his share of my love—
so why do I still stop and turn my head?

Summer Diet

That two-pound bag of pretzels in the kitchen
calls out in vain for me to plunge my hands in,
and with my study door closed I can't hear
the tin-foil muffled cries of chocolate cake
begging to be let out of the icebox
or the whimperings of peanut M&Ms,
trapped inside the cat-shaped candy jar
meant to discourage nibbling by mice,
to please come lift its lid and scoop them up.
All voices in the house are swallowed by
the purring of the central air conditioner
inhaling August and puffing out October.
It's 68 in here; I'm shivering,
though outside it's so hot that the cicadas
ceaselessly sing chainsaw arias.
It's easy to learn how they make that racket:
"Vibrating membranes under their abdomens,"
but why do their small bellies scream so loudly?
Is it because, though hungry, they refuse
to stuff themselves with green, delicious leaves,
preferring to slim down to hollow shells,
golden brown, glued to the bark of trees?
Or are they so tormented by the heat
that they cry to the birds, "Come! Eat me!"
Either way, they sing my belly's song:
deeper than the instinct to survive
must run the instinct to be cool and thin;
we won't shut up until we're skeletons.

Oona

One hot, polluted day by Lake Geneva,
the famous view I'd ridden an express train
to take in was enshrouded by gray smog,
so I decided not to walk the quay
I'd planned to walk since I read *Daisy Miller*
half my life before. But when I turned,
the automatic train door slammed against me,
stranding me in town at least an hour.
I shrugged and wove through the square-turned-parking-lot
down to the lake, arriving years too late
to see "Alps starkly rise from the far shore,"
as my out-of-print Baedeker said they did.
A century'd passed since Henry James's Daisy,
an ignorant American, drew stares
from stuffy Europeans when she strolled
unescorted past luxury hotels
like a prostitute—"adventuress" James would say.
If she returned and stepped into my shoes—
my rubber sandals, all the rage that year—
she'd still have recognized geraniums
festooning window boxes at The Grande,
and shoreline swans patrolling for thrown crumbs.
But she'd turn heads no more, not even twirling
her parasol and hobbling in a hoop skirt.
Too many thronged that walk for anyone's
weird costume or behavior to draw stares.
Roller skaters threaded the dense crowd
that pushed toward the entrance of the Casino,
whose marquee proclaimed in ten-foot letters:
"First Annual Country And Western Festival."
Of course the organizers got it wrong—
teepees on the lawn, and a paint pony
you could mount to have your picture taken.
The listed country singers with French names

like Jules and Jacques, who must've given up
on rock and roll when Hank Williams Jr.
grossed more in one night than The Stones in three,
were bound to mispronounce words like "Kentucky."
As people jostled by me, some for the show
and some for Texas Chile at the Chuckwagon
run by a squaw in a buckskin-fringed bikini,
it crossed my mind to buy a thirty-franc ticket
to listen to them mangle "Country Roads."
But pressure from the surging crowd dislodged me
and carried me like flotsam down the shoreline
to a grassy plot, where, shoved off the walk,
I bumped into a small man with a cane,
who sullenly said nothing to my "pardon."
Then I stepped back and saw that he was bronze—
a perfect full-sized cast of Charlie Chaplin.
I bowed and tipped my imaginary bowler,
then bent to read the inscription in his base,
which praised him as the town's most famous clown—
buried up the hill next to his villa.
With half an hour to kill, I decided
to make the pilgrimage. Beyond the yachts,
five-star hotels gave way to blocks of flats,
and the boulevard became a six-lane highway.
That's where my map showed Chaplin's cemetery,
but all I found was a tourist shopping mall.
I paced its asphalt, glancing at cuckoo clocks
in souvenir shop windows, which all agreed
I had just fifteen minutes till the train.
Then, uphill, I spied the graveyard's gate
with stairs cut in its wall that led up to it.
I hustled up them, pushed my way inside.
Luckily, not many dead lay there,
and no one living walked the gravel paths.
A showy patch of pink geraniums
like neon drew me to twin headstones: Charles
and his wife Oona, born thirty-six years later.

I'd never heard of her. His second or third?
Her grave was fresh. Eighteen years before,
she stood where I stood for his funeral,
glanced up at blue sky over bluer water,
and thought . . . god knows what. Free at last?
or Please don't make me live too long without him?
Or maybe she thought nothing, just watched a steamer
back out of the harbor and nose around,
as I did then, taking in the harbor.
The boat cut through the Styx-gray water
into haze. Swiss flags strung from its safety railings
waved as gaily as the jostling throng on deck.
I spotted Daisy Miller's ostrich hat,
still vivid since it was preserved in fiction,
and celluloid-thin Charlie in black and white.
But Oona—which one was she? The same age now
as all the famous dead, she'd disappeared
inside the smoke of the twentieth century.
She'd seen the world, like her, grow old and ugly
in spite of its pile of American money. HOOT
the steamer howled, which told me I had missed
the 4:15 to France. Then it vanished
into ghost-colored, man-made fog that made
its crossing to Oblivion perilous.

Ghosts in the Kitchen

Ouch! That hurts! I yelled when kitty nipped
my ankle as I washed her empty dish.
I shook my finger at her upraised face,
but she ducked beneath my robe again and probed
for my Achilles tendon with her fangs.
Waltzing out of range, I lectured her:
You're slowing down, not speeding up your breakfast!
I can't spoon out your Friskies while I'm dancing.
She paused to listen long enough for me
to fill her plastic dish with chicken bits
and slap it down and jump out of her way.
She snorted with delight and scarfed it up.
You like that, eh? I said and made a note
on my kitchen grocery list to buy this kind
next time I shopped instead of Science Diet,
which she turned her nose up at the day before.
I knelt and begged her to try just one bite:
Eat this, sweetie pie—It's good for you!
But when I heard my pleading voice, I shivered—
my long-dead mother reappeared before me
speaking those words in that same pleading tone
when I was six, and wouldn't touch my oatmeal.
I hate it! I screamed—*I want Sugar Pops!*
She sighed and dumped my breakfast in the sink,
promised me she'd buy the kind I wanted
the next time she shopped at the grocery store.
I want them now! I shouted and stalked out,
first snatching half a dozen Oreos
from her cookie jar. *Ungrateful jerk,*
I muttered as my sullen kid's face faded,
replaced by the sweet face of my blue Persian.
Oh, not you, Kitty, you're a perfect kitty,
I said and scrunched her ears until she ducked
and slinked into her corner for a nap.

Now look—today she's eaten all her breakfast
including one or two small nips of me,
and she's eager for her pill mashed in cream cheese.
Oh, what a good kitty you are, Kitty, I say
loud enough to recall my laughing mother,
younger than I am now, and mocking me.

Roots

In Italy this old money
tucked into my bedstand drawer
with my first passport, long expired,
got taken out of circulation
between my first and second visit
so that the change I didn't leave
on the table for the waiters
on my honeymoon in Venice
had turned into a souvenir
when I returned and tried to spend it
decades later in Palermo.
No Sicilian bank or store
or petty thief would take these bills
the color and size of Monopoly dollars
that once bought cups of cappuccino.
Think of flying home with money
that the airport shuttle driver
gave as change when you took off
but shook his head and handed back
on the day that you returned.
You'd have to find a VISA-taking
Airport Limo to ride home in,
and the sock you stuffed with dollars
and hid inside your dresser drawer
might as well have gotten stolen
by the burglar who broke in.
At least it would've stemmed his craving
for crack cocaine a day or two
instead of turning into worthless
portraits of George Washington.
But money in the U.S.A.'s
so durable that the first dollar
I ever earned, if I'd framed it
instead of buying fries and a shake,

would still pay for two hamburgers
on Wednesday Special at McDonald's,
and nickels are worth bending for
except when my back's acting up.
Even the pennies that I'd lay
on streetcar tracks for trolley cars
to mash flat when I was a child
are valuable enough to fish
from my pants pockets to make change
while customers, lined up behind me
at the check out, cough and shuffle.
Money's why my mother's father
sailed in steerage from Palermo
to Baltimore, where I grew up
and fled the first day that I could—
a city equally as ugly
and dangerous, I discovered
when I walked Palermo's streets
last year to find out what he'd left
when he'd fled from poverty
at the end of the nineteenth century.
The day he died his property
was worth enough for his ten children
to quarrel over its division
and never speak again. My mother,
the last to die, got not a penny.
I bought her funeral with money
made after fleeing Baltimore
and saved by never having children.
I stood beside her family plot
as she rejoined unspeaking brothers
and sisters and her bitter parents,
then drove all day at highway speed
to put that awful town behind,
but as I aimed into the sun,
thoughts of where I came from plagued me.
"I'm flying to Sicily," I said,

and did, taking these worthless lire
I didn't spend on my honeymoon.
That's the end of this immigrant's story:
I won't go back for love or money.

Happy Birthday, Richard!

Born in March, like a spring lamb, I learned
that life keeps getting better. Outside my window,
dead-stick branches bloomed and filled with birds
that kitty watched perched on my radiator,
which hissed and thumped less and less each day
as the sun rose earlier and shined more brightly.
At three months old, I'd blink and nights were gone.
I'd wake past dawn, shriek and get fed at once—
no more howling in the freezing dark.
Scented air blew in through open windows.
I was almost satisfied. Then things went wrong.
Lightning cracked the sky; the branches writhed;
They slammed my window shut against the rain.
Afterwards, the sky grew paler blue.
Every day, less sun and fewer birds.
And then the leaves turned brown and blew away,
the radiator hissed and thumped again,
and kitty, curled up on it, slept all day.
Is this what the rest of my life will be like?
I wailed as I writhed under tons of blankets
after waking in the middle of the night.
And then things started to go right again—
more heat, more light. One day the people lit
a candle in a cupcake as they sang,
"Happy Birthday, Richard." I was one.
The bad times were behind me, spring ahead,
all the butter icing I could eat—
what more could I want? But I was tense.
Sure, spring was coming, and summer guaranteed,
but that meant winter, too, was on the way.
Half the time, I'd shiver in the dark,
the other half, I'd know the happiness
bubbling through my veins and nerves was doomed.
"Blow your candle, baby, make a wish!"

I pursed my lips and feebly blew the flame,
wishing I were one day old again,
ignorant, about to enter spring.
That was fifty-seven years ago today;
I'm celebrating spring's rebirth again,
my futile wish still fanning unquenched flames,
with icing for consolation—plus iced champagne,
which makes me feel I'm one day old again.

The Diver

Snorkeling in three-thousand-foot-deep water
off the coastline of a live volcano,
I realized I'd never take up diving
as a metaphor for plumbing *my* unconscious.
My darkest depths lie so near the surface
I'd hit myself in the face if I plunged in
the deepest pool of my desires and fears.
Mirrored in water, my image doesn't lure me
towards it for a Narcissistic kiss;
in fact, I duck away from my reflection,
just as I duck down towards the water fountain
when I spot someone in the hall at work
in order to avoid having to say,
Hi! What's up? How's it going? Fine!
I'm Okay, You're Okay's my policy
both on the job and at home after work,
even waking in the dark from dreams
more vivid than real life. I'd rather not
know more about my dream self, always drowning
or falling backwards off of fire truck ladders
or running through molasses, fleeing tigers
or searching desperately for discharge papers
to show to MPs pounding on the door
who've come to drag me back into the army.
Sure, now and then there's sex with eager strangers,
or I complete the doctoral dissertation
that I abandoned twenty years ago
and am finally awarded a PhD,
or, best of all, my buoyant body soars
when I stretch out my arms to catch the breeze.
But waking from such pleasant dreams is painful—
falling back to earth, weighted down
by lead reality. That's my kind of diving—
sinking to the surface of my mattress

so far below the ceiling of my dreams
that it seems, for a second, like the depths.
But then I feel the tug of gravity
that wants to sink me six feet into earth,
and I feel grateful for my Beauty Rest,
which cradles me like this smooth, salty water
three-fifths of a mile above the bottom
where blind fish fin their way through the dark
below the simple appetites of sharks.

Final Exercise—The Rain Poem

for my students

It's raining torrents on the Interstate
that I'm not speeding towards home on tonight
dodging semis hauling freight to Memphis.
Evening Classics isn't fading out
fifty miles south of West Lafayette,
so I'm not reaching towards my dial to search
by Braille for *Pipe Dreams'* doleful organ music
beamed fifty miles north out of Bloomington
while I merge one-handed with Indy Beltway's drunks,
who aren't roaring past me, flinging spray
then slowing down to weave in front of me
while lighting smokes that won't cut short their lives—
slow death in bed of cancer's not their fate.
Construction pylons aren't squeezing traffic
from three lanes into mine before I exit
to State Road 67, woods-lined and dark,
where deer who lurk behind the trees preparing
to involve me in their suicide attempts
are about to feel a poignant disappointment.
All eight convenience stores that light my path
through Martinsville might just as well extinguish
signs boasting of cheap gas and cigarettes
and give that town back to its primal darkness.
I'm not resuming speed now past the drive-in
whose marquee lost its letters years ago,
and even if I were, Orion's stars—
the only constellation that I know
besides the Dipper—wouldn't fill the sky
I'd glimpse when I glanced left to check for cops
before I pushed my pedal to the floor.
No, all I'd see's a uniform bright gray
lit from below by distant city lights

refracted through cascades of falling droplets.
So my spirits wouldn't lift because the sword-star
seemed to point toward my distant house
as if put there by Zeus for just that purpose.
Instead, I'd think the rain was trying to kill me
by hydroplaning my worn Michelins—
worn from 15 weeks of this commuting
to teach a night creative writing workshop
to students who, now, aren't getting soaked
as they trudge home alone to their apartments
from the dim bar where they meet after class
to criticize critiques. No, they're in bed, asleep,
or else they're listening to the rhythm of the rain
while staring at their blank computer screens,
delighting in making something out of nothing
exactly like me and without my help.

November's Advice

Counselors call this feeling you are feeling,
staring through gray drizzle at bare branches
with, here and there, a yellow leaf still clinging,
"seasonal depression" which they'll cure
with Prozac if you can afford it. If not,
then what you've got's the blues because you're poor.
In that case your best remedy is heroin,
for which they can not write you a prescription,
or Gallo wine, which does not require one.
But what if what you've guessed just now is true—
your life's changed nothing, not even for the worse;
the Earth does not require the work you do?
What's the cure for being superfluous?
"Redundant—cut" your English teacher wrote
in the wide margins of your padded essays
because you really had nothing to say.
Counselors can't tell you "go cut your throat,"
but isn't that what they mean to imply
when they urge you to "just take it easy"?
Every useless thing is saying, "die!"—
the drones, belly up on the window sill,
the window-bashing, suicidal flies.
Why mask this feeling with a costly pill?
You are worthless, and your work is futile.

Flying Home

When the boy next door's father traded
his Chevy for a Pontiac
and moved from our brick row-house block,
I pitied him for being exiled.
Our neighborhood was ugly, yes,
but so near our city's heart
that Downtown buses rocked me to sleep
and stirred up diesel-scented breezes
on sultry, airless nights in summer.
I could walk, in half an hour,
to Branch 10 and Branch 15
of the Enoch Pratt Free Library
and check out twice my five-book limit,
and the stadium was so nearby
that, playing stickball in the alley
with the kids from down the street,
I could hear the home crowd cheering.
Silence meant our team was losing;
a roar meant we'd just hit a home run,
or, in fall, that our quarterback
had thrown a long bomb for a touchdown.
Now and then a cheer would rise
just after I had knocked the ball
over the rusty chain-link fence.
Then I'd wave my broomstick bat
acknowledging the fans' applause
while my playmates laughed and razzed.
But one by one they moved away
to split levels in the suburbs.

In winter, tired of solitaire,
I built forts out of decks of cards,
then nuked them with spring-loaded missiles—
Free in Every Box of Cheerios!

95

On summer afternoons I'd read
German U-Boat captains' memoirs
and tales of teenage stowaways
on rockets cruising distant space—
my longing for the womb, I guess,
or maybe just my deep desire
to cram myself into a capsule
speeding far from loneliness
to diamond necklace galaxies
ten zillion light years from my house.
So when I boarded my first flight,
a silver Trans-World Airline jet,
one-way, coast-to-coast, nonstop,
I felt as if I'd flown before
when the engines roared and thrust me
deep into my padded seat.
As the pilot banked our wings,
I saw spread out for miles below
the suburbs lucky friends had moved to—
polished cars and swimming pools
flashing in the setting sun.
For half a second I regretted
not having fled our rotting city's
center for this sparkling fringe
where, I guess, those friends still live
raising children of their own.
But then our Boeing's cabin tipped
and climbed full-thrust toward the stars
just winking on above the wings.
And by the time we banked again
to circle San Francisco Bay—
a black hole ringed by golden lights,
just like the galaxies I'd dreamed—
the only thing that I regretted
was our necessity to land.

Twenty First Century Blues

Why should I live now? I wondered,
when Carol Anne announced to us
her father had been transferred South,
which wrecked my plans to marry her
in fifteen years and buy a row house
exactly like the ones we lived in
and raise a couple of kids like us.
Suppressing sobs, I asked my playmates,
"what's your favorite century?"
For why not live some other time
beginning with the dinosaurs
and ending with the Last Judgment
raining fire on all our houses,
burning up our dogs and cats
who wouldn't get to go to Heaven.
Already I'd reached double figures,
ten years old and brokenhearted,
failing Penmanship and Conduct.
I might not ever get promoted
to fourth grade books with smaller print
and characters with darker thoughts
than Dick and Jane and Puff and Spot.
I'd have to waste my whole existence
rounding out my big G's loops
and learning to keep my mouth shut.
But even if my third grade teacher
got rid of me with a gift C-,
my future looked too desolate
with Carol Anne ripped out of it.
I wished that I could travel back
before my misery was born.
Since history wasn't my best subject—
the only era I knew well
was "yesteryear" when The Lone Ranger

roamed the plains with his friend Tonto—
I turned to my friends Cal and Jack,
both experts on the pre-cowboy past.
"I'd like to wear the lace and velvet
of Louis XIV's court at Versailles,"
said Jack, who was into fabrics
so deep he helped his older sister
cut patterns for her dresses out.
"Give me Nero's Rome," said Cal,
fond of pulling legs off bugs,
who'd seen *Quo Vadis* three times
and said he rooted for the lions
when Caesar flung the Christians to them
in the first Olympic games.
But Carol Anne, whose blue eyes stared
like x-rays through me and my friends,
looked as if she'd moved already
to a future that excluded us.
At last she tossed her curls and said,
"What does it matter when we live?
By 2000 we'll be fifty
and you'll have all forgotten me."
Then she stood tip-toe on saddle shoes,
pirouetted, marched away
down Argonne Drive, out of my life,
but not out of my memory
for the remnant of our century,
or the small piece of the next one
left before I have to die.